PRENTICE HALL 22.95

RIVERS AND LAKES

SIMON & SCHUSTER

LONDON • SYDNEY • NEW YORK • TOKYO • SINGAPORE • TORONTO

First Published in 1991 by
Simon & Schuster Young Books
Simon & Schuster Ltd
Wolsey House
Wolsey Road
Hemel Hempstead
Hertfordshire HP2 4SS
England

British Library Cataloguing in Publication Data

Knapp, Brian
Rivers and Lakes (Caring for environments)
1. Rivers and Lakes – Juvenile literature
I. Title II. Series
551.48

ISBN 0-7500-0842-3

Printed and bound in Hong Kong

Author Dr. Brian Knapp
Illustrators Tim Smith and Mark Franklin
Designed and produced by
EARTHSCAPE EDITIONS,
86 Peppard Road,
Sonning Common, Reading,
Berkshire, RG4 9RP, UK

Picture credits

t=top b=bottom l=left r=right

All photographs from the Earthscape Editions photographic library except the following: The Hutchchison Library – Front Cover, 36t; USGS 35; ZEFA 21t, 30, 43t

CONTENTS

1: WHAT ARE RIVERS?

Rivers – natural channels that carry water from the land to the sea – are a vital lifeline for all the people of the world. Rivers provide water for drinking, water for crops, a way of cooling machines and power stations, and a cheap means of transport, as well as an inexhaustible source of raw materials.

Rivers and lakes are such common words, but people around the world often have very different images of what they are. People who live in well-watered regions think of rivers with wide sweeping curves and gentle flow. They think of tree-lined banks and places to swim or fish. People who live in the mountains think of shallow cascades with rocks and rapids and waterfalls. Those who live in drier regions are used to rivers drying up each year. And those near the sea or on the world's biggest rivers and lakes think of them as waterways for carrying goods and building ports.

Because rivers and lakes provide fresh water they have always drawn people to their banks. But people have rarely been content to leave nature alone. For a river that brings drinking water also brings floods and danger; it brings silt, sand and stones, it carves out the banks and is endlessly on the move.

People have always tried to harness their rivers, to straitjacket them and stop them from behaving naturally. Sometimes it seems that they have had some success; in other cases the same techniques have brought total disaster.

Most of the world's cities *have been constructed on rivers, many – such as Pittsburgh, USA, shown here – have grown because of their trading position at the junction or confluence of two navigable rivers. People are therefore often anxious to make the most use of this valuable resource.*

Rivers can be deceptive. *For much of the year they can appear slow moving and calm. But they can also flood their banks and cause great destruction for those unwise enough to live too close.*

How people have lived with rivers and lakes, the mistakes they have made, and the way they can leave them for future generations to enjoy depends on understanding how rivers and lakes work. The natural processes that work in rivers and lakes is described in the first part of this book. The second part looks at the many ways people use rivers and lakes, the battles they have had with nature, their successes and failures. We will find how the pressure from people often puts at risk the very rivers and lakes they need. The last section shows how we can look after our water even in places where there are severe demands.

Lakes turn speedy rivers into quiet deep pools. *They are the equalisers of the river's system, soaking up the floods and providing water when there is no rain. They also provide leisure opportunities.*

Pattern in rivers

At first you might think that the world's rivers are very different from each other. The Amazon, for example, is deep, even-flowing and often clear. By contrast, the Nile swells when rains pour down on its mountain source, and then dwindles to a trickle as the dry season sets in. The Hwang He is quite different again. It is called the Yellow River because it often looks like liquid cement as it carries soil eroded from the nearby hills.

But these are relatively small differences, for these giant rivers share much in common with each other and even with the small rivers that flow in every valley. They have sources in distant hills, they flow in channels and their waters are swollen by the additions from many tributaries.

***Water evaporating from the sea**, making clouds, rain and snow begins the never-ending water cycle which feeds all the world's rivers and lakes.*

Rain or snow seeps into the soil and moves downhill until the soil becomes saturated. Water then spills onto the surface creating the sources of rivers. From then on the water runs in a channel on the surface, joining with other channels until it reaches the sea, perhaps being slowed down occasionally by the presence of lakes.

The pattern carved by rivulets on a bare hillside shows all the same characteristics of the Amazon, but on a miniature scale. The main channel sets the scene, carving a trench to which all the tributaries cut down. Soil slips down slopes to the channels, opening out the land into patterns of valleys with smoothly sloping sides. The channels spread over the land, eating headwards until they find competition from some nearby river system, then growing and branching until they form a dense network of water courses that can carry water swiftly and evenly from the land after it has fallen as rain.

A stable river system has branches that look like the roots of a tree, or the veins in a human body. Each is part of a network and all have become finely tuned to carry water effectively from the river basin. If people understand how finely balanced this system is, then they will soon see that a change made in one place can have repercussions everywhere else – many of them quite unforeseen.

2: RIVER SOURCES

Whatever its length or size, a river will always have a source and carry water to a mouth. However, in between, the nature of the river is much less certain. The river may erode, deposit, break up into many channels, reform, and twist about. It may cascade over rapids or waterfalls, or it may sink into the deep still waters of a lake. It may disappear underground and re-emerge many kilometres away.

Each part of a river that has the same type of flow and which shapes the same kind of channel and valley is called a **reach**. Very often there are three main types of reach, an upper reach, where the river is not much larger than the tributaries that flow into it and where the river often tumbles over a rock-strewn bed; a middle reach, where a main stream dominates the landscape and where the river flows in a channel that is lined with fine sediment, and a lower reach, where the river moves slowly towards its mouth in a wide, almost level landscape.

The majority of rivers *begin in dips in the land where water seeps in from surrounding soils. Such rivers swell rapidly when storms occur because the soils cannot store much of the water. They also dry up quickly in periods without rain for the same reasons. Rivers that go from high to low flow quickly are called* ***flashy****. They are the most likely to flood.*

Sources of rivers

River sources are illusive. Although a river may appear to form from a spring, for example, the water to make the spring has filtered down through soil and rock and perhaps already made a journey of many kilometres.

Soils hold the main sources of river water because they act like a sponge, soaking up the rainwater and holding it in minute gaps called **soil pores**. As each new supply of rainwater flows in, so it pushes the water already in the pores deeper. Sometimes the water seeps into rocks and from here seeps to rivers. A rock – such as limestone – that stores and transmits water is called an **aquifer**. Rocks can store far more water than soils, so if they occur they are a vital steadying influence on river flow.

Many rocks are not aquifers and then the water must flow to the rivers through the soils or over the surface. Soils cannot easily cope with the water from a severe storm and rivers without aquifers are far more likely to flood.

Most of the largest rivers in the world start from humble beginnings where soil water seeps to the surface as a spring. Only occasionally there is a more dramatic source, such as a snowfield or a glacier melting when large amounts of water are released. If they do have this special supply, streams can quickly become substantial rivers.

This river is emerging *from below a melting glacier. Under the ice the glacier has eroded large amounts of rock which the river can use to* ***abrade*** *(scrape away) at its bed. Glacier-fed rivers have a much more powerful beginning than most rivers.*

A few rivers are fed *by underground springs. This usually happens in limestone regions. Here you can see a river emerging at the foot of a limestone cliff. The land on the cliff top has no surface drainage.*

***River beds tell a clear story** for those with the knowledge to interpret them. This picture shows a small stream channel littered with large boulders. When these boulders move they crash into each other and abrade small fragments off each other, a process called attrition. In this way boulders get smaller as they move towards the sea.*

How rivers erode

Rivers are at their most spectacular when they are tumbling over mountain rocks or cascading down waterfalls. Yet curiously enough this is also the time when they are most at the mercy of the landscape. They do not have the power to sweep out wide plains and make their own course. Instead the waters fall over themselves in a chaotic manner following the land shape that has been fashioned by the mountains.

Rivers get their cutting power from the debris they carry. This is why storms are so vital to landscape change. It is only when a river swells that it has the energy to pick up the stones that otherwise lie scattered across its bed.

Tools for erosion

Water alone is not good at eroding rocks. It may dissolve limestone, but otherwise it is almost powerless. But a river armed with stones to throw at its bed and banks is quite another matter.

A typical selection of water-rounded pebbles

Pot holes mark the places *where the stream uses pebbles to drill into its bed. During a storm eddies in the water swirl pebbles round and round until they erode the bed and form a pot hole. As pot holes wear into each other they deepen the bed.*

Pot holes are only seen in the upper reaches of fast flowing rivers where the energy in the water is sufficient to carry all the sediment away. In the lower reaches of a river the bed is usually masked by sediment and pot holes do not form.

With these stones it can tear soil and rock from its banks and wear down its bed, processes which cause abrasion. This is why a single big storm might cause more change than a thousand years of quiet water.

You can get a good idea of the storm power of a river by looking at the largest stones in its bed. These boulders hammer the bed when they move, creating fine chips of rock which are more easily carried away by the water. When enough fine **sediment** is on the move it changes the colour of the water. What colour it becomes depends on the material being carried.

No two rivers *have the same erosive power. Here at the junction, or confluence, of two rivers of about the same size you can see how one is almost white from the amount of sediment it is carrying, whereas the other is clear and blue.*

Waterfalls and rapids

Deep dark canyons, rapids and waterfalls are the marks of rivers that are cutting down swiftly through the rocks.

As the river cuts down so swiftly, landslides and rockfalls keep the valley sides bare and unstable. It is easy to see why the type of rock plays an important part in shaping the landscape. Hard, tough rocks make craggy, almost vertical valley sides, while softer rocks give steep rubble-covered slopes.

When rivers cut into hard and soft rocks that have been laid horizontally one above the other they often cause waterfalls. In places where they tilt the contrasts in rocks show up as rapids and **cataracts**.

Not all waterfalls and rapids are the result of river action. Some may be due to events in the recent geological past. Many mountain waterfalls cascade down the sides of valleys that have been gouged out by glaciers.

Elsewhere, Earth movements have pushed one part of the Earth's crust higher than another to form cliffs over which rivers tumble.

***Waterfalls**, cascades and rapids all occur on the Yellowstone River. Here a bar of particularly tough volcanic rock produces the spectacular waterfall. Elsewhere groups of soft rocks are being eroded quickly, but the hard bands take longer. As water tumbles over the tough rocks it forms into rapids with more energy for erosion.*

The 'white' water that marks a rapid shows where the river energy is concentrated on the hard rocks. The rapids never disappear, but by concentrating energy, river processes can be made to erode these hard rocks at the same rate as the rest of the river bed.

Why waterfalls retreat

Hard rock bands that lie horizontally across the river's path hold up downcutting until they can be undermined, broken into manageable-sized rubble and washed away.

As the water falls over the top surface or lip it speeds up and hits the bottom with great force. Rocks carried over the lip are swirled round with the water to erode a deep pool called a plunge pool.

As the plunge pool gets bigger it begins to undercut the softer rocks of the waterfall face leaving the hard rocks overhanging.

Many waterfalls *are accidents of geological history. Here, the Nevada Falls spills over the lip of a glaciated valley in Yosemite National Park, USA. There has not even been time to form a plunge pool or to undercut the valley. As a result the waterfall is more like a huge water slide.*

Niagara Falls*, on the US/Canadian border, is one of the world's largest waterfalls. The top layer of rock is a kind of hard limestone called dolomite. Beneath it are the softer rocks of shale and sandstone. As these softer rocks are scoured away the dolomite is left unsupported, until it finally falls away to make the rubble that fringes the base of the fall.*

3: RIVERS AND VALLEYS

As a stream moves further from its source and becomes substantial enough to earn the title 'river', the flowing water begins to play an increasingly important role in shaping the channel and the valley in which it flows.

However, a river can only cut a channel appropriate to its flow – it could never directly cut a valley. Rather, it cuts a deep channel, a kind of slot in the landscape which – if it were not balanced by valley widening – would become a gorge. Gorges are common in upland rivers near sources because the river is still far from its mouth and the reach is very steep.

The valley widens

Widening is the result of a combination of frost, heat and rain which break down, or weather the rock into smaller loose fragments of stones or soil. This material then rolls, slides or creeps down to the river.

Any valley shape is a balance between the cutting of the river bed and the widening of the valley by weathering. If the river cuts faster than new debris can be produced by weathering the valley sides are steep or even gorge-like. If, on the other hand, the speed of cutting by

Valleys may take many thousands of years to form *but in the process huge volumes of rock and soil have to be moved. In places such as this steep-sided valley the soil is frequently stripped by landslides. This provides an unstable home for trees and they are often toppled over by landslides and thrown into the river. This explains why there are patches of valley without soil and why most trees are so small and young.*

A river that is cutting down quickly can be identified by the straight slopes that lead from river bank to hill top. There is no flat land beside the channel.

Where the slopes are more gentle *boulders are nowhere to be seen. Here there is time for the rock to be weathered into soil and for the soil to* ***creep*** *imperceptibly to the banks or to be carried away in solution. But there is still no flat land beside the river.*

the river is more than matched by the weathering of the valley sides, the valley widens. This usually occurs when a river has moved to a gentler landscape and where the chances of downcutting by the river is lessened.

A valley is formed when there is more of a balance between the downcutting of the river and the processes such as landslides and soil creep that change the slopes.

At this stage it begins the process of swinging from side to side in the valley – cutting into some banks and drifting away from others. A surprisingly regular pattern is produced, each bend being separated by alternating spurs of land in the valley. These are known as interlocking spurs. However, valley sides are still steep and there are no large areas of flat land of the kind you would expect near a lowland river.

Flat land beside a river is called a flood plain. It is not cut by the river, but rather it has been deposited in layers each time the river flooded. It is a sign that the river is not powerful enough to carry away all the materials that reach its banks. A floodplain is a kind of temporary dumping ground, a place where sediment is stored between floods.

Notice that the valley slopes are very gentle. With the river spending so much of its energy carrying sediment there is little left to cut the bed deeper and so there is plenty of time for valley slopes to weather into gentler forms.

Floodplains

Lowland rivers have a lot of energy for erosion, but they cannot use it to cut downwards or the channel will become too gentle to transport the water and sediment. Instead the energy is used in eroding sideways and in the formation of a wide, flat floor.

The wide, flat floor of a valley is called a floodplain. This is the part of the valley that usually floods during a large storm when the river channels cannot handle all the water from upstream.

Floodwater does not flow as fast as water in a channel. This means it cannot continue to carry the coarsest – and therefore heaviest – materials such as gravel and sand. These are deposited on the banks where they sometimes build up to form broad natural walls. These are called levees. The finer material is washed on further because it settles out of the water only slowly. As the flood abates and the water level falls. Much of this fine material gets left on the floodplain. After each flood, therefore, the valley floor gets another tiny layer of sediment added to its surface. Over thousands of years it is this that forms the bulk of the floodplain.

During a flood *the river water turns brown because of the large volume of fine silt and clay being carried. Water spilling from the river onto the floodplain encounter many obstacles such as trees and bushes. These act as a brake on the flow of water and, as it slows down it deposits the sediment as a thin layer.*

***This aerial view of a river** shows how it twists across its flood plain. In many places it is held in its course by trees (which show as a dark green colour). Where there are no trees the banks are eroding quickly (white colour). Notice how some bends are tight and have sharp bends, others seem to curl more gently. A river is never a place of neat meanders where each one is the same as the next.*

The importance of storms

Storms also produce dramatic changes in the river channel. The normal twists and turns of a river (called meanders) are obstacles to the free flow of storm water and they help cause early flooding.

Tight bends are especially troublesome to fast flow and during floods many rivers 'pond up' behind a tight bend, spill over the top and cut a new, shorter channel. In time the old channel bend is abandoned, forming a banana-shaped pond sometimes called an oxbow lake. Meanwhile the river channel moves to a new place on its floodplain.

***This tree is growing on an outside bend** where deep water allows very fast flow in times of flood. You can see how the water has scoured away the soil from beneath the tree so it now appears to be standing on stilts.*

Meanders and braids

Rivers twist and turn in definite patterns. In some places a river might twist and turn as a single channel as we saw on the previous page. This is called meandering, and each of the curves is known as a meander. Meanders will always be found in floodplains where fine materials occur.

In other places there may be no well defined single channel, but the river appears to wander in many channels, each divided by a gravel or sand island. This pattern, common in areas with coarse floodplain materials is called braiding, and each of the small channels is called a braid.

***This river seems to be rushing out of control**, spilling first this way, then that. In some places it divides and leaves islands, at others it widens and then narrows.*

These are all the characteristics of a river flowing over sand and gravel. There is no clay to help hold the banks together because the river is flowing too fast for the clay to settle. This is a braided river, and each thread of the channel is a braid. This river (the River Rhone) is carrying the meltwaters of the Rhone glacier in Switzerland.

Braided streams are common where valley slopes are still steep, or in dry places where the debris to be carried is always coarse sand or gravel.

***The sweeping curves of this river** have been cut through several times in the recent past. They show on the inside bend where shallow water-filled channels occur. So far they have not produced a permanent change to the meander shape, but each new flood will cut the channels deeper and make a cut-off more likely.*

Slope is the key

Rivers seem to meander or braid in a bewildering variety of shapes and sizes. However, things are not quite as chaotic as they may seem. You only find braids on the steeper slopes of valleys for example.

There are also reasons for why a meander has a particular shape and size. This is because meanders have a purpose: they slow down the river flow. In just the same way as a twisted hose will make it harder to water a garden, so a meandering channel will act like a brake on the water, slowing it down so that it does not rush too quickly to its mouth.

Gentle rivers do not need brakes and so meanders are weak and ill-defined. But rivers flowing on steeper courses need the stabilizing effects of meanders more and more and steeper floodplains always have huge snaking meanders. Such rivers frequently cut off their own meanders during floods.

4: LAKES AND DELTAS

Lakes were not formed by rivers. They are some accident of the Earth's history. Many are the result of erosion by glaciers and ice sheets that once covered the land. In upland areas glacial scouring was so intense it often scooped out troughs in valleys. This picture of Ullswater in the English Lake District, is one such example. In lowlands lakes are often formed by the deposits left by ice sheets as they melted away. Lake Como in northern Italy is still held in place by a huge ridge (called a terminal **moraine**) which marks the farthest the Alpine ice sheets reached when they deposited their debris.

In North America, the sheer weight of an ancient ice sheet was enough to make the land sink into a basin. As the ice departed and water flowed over the land again it filled up the basin to form the Great Lakes – Huron, Michigan, Erie and others.

Huge movements deep within the Earth were needed to force parts of the crust to sink down to make the world's deepest lakes, like the USSR's Lake Baikal and the East African Rift Valley lakes such as Lake Albert.

***Some lakes occupy strange places**. Perhaps the strangest of all is high up in the top of a volcanic mountain on America's west coast. Oregon's Crater Lake lies 2000 metres above sea level and is nearly 700 metres deep. It was formed when the volcano erupted so violently that the top of the mountain was blown away, the rest sinking back in on itself to give a spectacular circular lake.*

***A delta forming** at one end of glacially scoured Derwentwater, England. The picture to the right shows how the delta is filling in one end of the lake.*

***The sediment that builds a delta** in a lake or a sea can form into many different patterns. The one shown here is often called a 'bird's foot' delta. The River Mississippi makes this kind of delta as it enters the Gulf of Mexico.*

In this picture you can see how the river runs over the delta it has made, thrusting ever further into the lake. But the river flows over a very gentle slope as it enters the lake and much sediment is dropped in the sluggish waters. Together these deposits build up the bed and banks until they are often much higher that the surroundings.

In times of flood it is common for the river to break out from its high bed and spill to left or right. You can see clearly where this has happened here. It is the constant breaking of banks that allows sediment to be deposited over a wide area and to make the characteristic triangular shape of a delta.

Deltas

When a river spills into a lake it enters a huge body of still water. Here the sediment that has been carried in the channel begins to settle out. As it does so, the sediment builds a new part to the landscape – a delta.

When you look at a delta, you can begin to see how much sediment the river carries. But you are just looking at the 'tip of an iceberg'. Below the water the delta spreads out its gently sloping sides. As the delta grows some distant hill is being worn down. Slowly but surely the delta will be the death of the lake.

Many lakes have filled in the past. They now make flat, featureless plains that make some of the best farmland in the world. Every lake will be filled some day – it is just a matter of time.

This is Dana Lake, *one of many lakes in Yosemite National Park, USA. All have been formed by the scouring action of a glacier. But the signs that the lake is silting up are all around. Look carefully and you can see the tree-lined lake edge is fringed with marsh plants. As these plants spread their roots into the lake they trap sediment and turn lake into land. In this way the lake is growing smaller and it will inevitably be filled in.*

The main valley of Yosemite was also once a lake*, but only the observant would now see its traces. The trees in the valley bottom are growing on a wide flat floor – a former lake bed. The valley was filled in long ago because many sediment-laden rivers converged from the surrounding mountains.*

5: RIVER LIFE

Below the surface of rivers and lakes lies a treasurehouse of wildlife. It is immensely varied because natural rivers and lakes offer a multitude of places for each species to thrive. There are shallows and pools, rapids and calms, rocky reaches and silty reaches, and pebbly beds and sandy ones. Each can provide just the right kind of home for a distinctive set of plants and animals.

A natural river, free of pollution, *can support a wide variety of plant life on its bed. In these crystal clear waters you can see a number of species of water plant, each adapted to survive in the swiftly flowing current. The darker-coloured species occupies the bed where the faster thread of water flows, while the lighter-coloured species thrives in less turbulent sites.*

Mountain streams gather their water *from seepages through their banks. Many small water-loving plants grow in this moist environment, creating the mountain meadow shown in this picture.*

Although it looks such a fertile environment, the plants you see are specially adapted for living in these cold and slightly acidic waters. True river plants need more nourishment than these waters can provide and few grow in such places. This is the reason it is so easy to see the bed.

The value of oxygen

Many **aquatic** creatures depend on the dissolved oxygen in the water. Aquatic plants constantly give out oxygen, while more is absorbed from the air. Colder water can hold more oxygen than warm, but animals are more active in warm waters and so in the summer months the need for a good supply of oxygen is important. It is at this time that a good speedy flow of turbulent water is vital to survival. Slow, sluggish rivers cannot absorb enough oxygen to support large amounts of wildlife.

Riverside plants have to survive *with their roots constantly in water. Many of them are specially adapted to extract oxygen from the water. Their mass of tangled roots helps them to withstand the battering of floodwaters. In turn the vegetation also stabilizes the river banks.*

Adapting

Water-loving plants have to be able to thrive in widely varying flows. Those which choose the faster waters of the outside meander bend often have long streaming fronds that are splayed out by the water like flags in a breeze. They need to be firmly anchored to the bed and they have long, tough roots.

Riverbank trees must protect themselves against erosion by sinking strong roots deep into the soil.

These tough survivors have a big effect on the river. They stabilize the banks, and tend to fix the channel for longer in one place. A floodplain with natural vegetation along its banks is far less likely to change course than one that has nothing.

By contrast, the inside banks of rivers offer calm conditions where less sturdy plants can colonize. **Eddies** from the fast outer bank bring fine particles onto the inside where they can be trapped by reeds and other plants. In this way what is lost from one bank is gained by the other and the river's width stays constant.

Wildlife survival

The plants of the water and bank provide the food for such animals as sticklebacks and some insect larvae (the herbivores) which are eaten in turn by the hunters such as pike, heron or bears (carnivores). Together with the creatures that eat dead plants and animals (the decomposers), they make up the water pattern of life called an **ecosystem**.

Plants are important for food, but they also provide shelter against hunters and the materials for nests. The branches of trees that overhang water make ideal perches for birds before they dive into the water to catch their prey.

Bears are spectacular hunters. *They stand quietly in the clear waters of a river and wait for the sight of a fish in the water below. As a fish passes they make swift movements with their powerful claws. This bear is trying to catch a salmon as it leaps over rapids on its way to its spawning grounds.*

Wildlife survival depends on there being just the right balance of plants, herbivores, carnivores and decomposers. However, this balance can be so easily disrupted by people. Natural lake edges have swampy margins where reeds grow; often they are cleared away to provide a better view for people, but in doing so they deprive some wild creatures of their natural home, or habitat. Clearly wildlife will not survive if too much of their **habitat** is destroyed.

Rivers provide a multitude of habitats for creatures. Some thrive in the fast flowing thread of current that runs near the centre of the channel; others need the shelter of the inside bends or the deep pools on the outer bend. These conditions can easily be destroyed in rivers that are straightened and their shape made more regular.

Wildlife lives in a delicate balance; it is the most easily disrupted of all natural systems, but it is also the one which most competes with people for space in the world. This is why caring for environments is an especially important task, so that all can survive.

Trout have very specialized requirements. *They thrive best in fast flowing waters that have both pools and shallows. This is where they find the insects on which they feed. A healthy river can support a large number of trout, as this picture shows.*

Swans are some of the biggest water birds *outside of the Tropics. They eat both plants and insects. They live in shallow waters where they use their long necks to dredge in the mud of the channel bed. They also use reed beds and other marshy habitats to make secure, defendable nests and to rear their young.*

6: LIVING WITH RIVERS

If people are to enjoy living with rivers and lakes they have to understand how the natural environment works. Then they can decide how best to plan to work with the environment.

In the first part of this book we saw how, for the majority of the time river channels were big enough to carry all the water that seeped through their banks, but that large storms caused flooding.

We saw that river energy was used both to erode the bed and banks and to carry sediment to the sea. If lakes interrupted the course of a river, the sediment was deposited there, building outwards from deltas.

In places near to river sources the main action of the river was to cut down quickly, causing landslides and mud flows on the valley slopes. But further downstream the river changed to cutting mostly sideways, valley slopes became more gentle and a floodplain with a meandering channel was produced.

The variety of natural rivers has provided enormous scope for a great diversity of wildlife. There are turbulent and calm stretches, deep and shallow ones. Groups of species have become adapted to each of these special environments.

The effect of changes

In the past people learned from experience to live with the river. With hand tools, the populations of most countries were not able to change rivers to any significant extent, so they chose to live on the river's terms. If people wanted to be near to a river they chose the inside bend of a meander where it was safer

The advent of insurance and technology *has made people much more foolhardy in their use of riverbanks. You might think that nobody would seriously build a car park where the cars could get flooded. But this is just what is happening in more and more places. The owners ask the insurance company to pay for any damage due to floods, and they ask their local government officials to stop any future floods by building high river-bank walls.*

and their homes were not eroded by the river; they chose dry sites on land that was high above the river; and they chose natural crossing points where the river was broad and shallow and could be forded.

But as people became better engineers they grew dissatisfied with living on nature's conditions. Instead they chose more and more to modify rivers and lakes for their own purposes.

People's relationship with rivers has changed. *About a thousand years ago the church was built on a high, dry site clear of river floods. About two hundred years ago the dry sites were used up and a brewery (the buff-coloured building) had to be constructed on land that was still safe from all except the largest floods. Today luxury houses are being built right against the water's edge so the owners can have good views. But they will not be safe from even moderate floods.*

Bridges are essential *if people want to cross rivers. But most bridges are built like this one with piers in the middle of the river. Although this obstruction makes little difference in times of normal flow, during a flood water cannot get through this bridge opening fast enough and it backs up, causing greater flooding than if the bridge had not been built.*

Because it is convenient *to use river valleys as routeways through hills and mountains, people will often find a way of squeezing a road in beside a river. However, in times of flood there may not be room for both. This road was completely washed away in a severe storm in 1976 but it has been rebuilt on exactly the same spot as before.*

Among the first people who lived by rivers and lakes were farmers. They saw the changing mood of the water and they knew which were the safe and which were the hazardous places to build. But as populations grew in villages and towns changes had to be made. First, the highest and driest sites were used up, so that if people wanted to live in the chosen settlement they were forced to use a place that was less satisfactory for their home. Then people often came from far and wide to swell the towns. These people had no knowledge of the natural environment, and so they could not easily judge the mood of the rivers.

This river is cutting rapidly *into the landscape and the slopes are very unstable. This is not a good place to build houses because they are liable to be carried away by landslides. The weight of the buildings may even make sliding more likely.*

Big Thompson

Big Thompson is a mountain river that will be remembered for a long time by people in the Rocky Mountains of the USA. On a summer's evening in 1976 a huge rainstorm gathered over the mountain and dumped over 25 centimetres of water on the land in four brief hours. It was more than the thin soils could take and water was soon spilling over the surface and swelling the river.

The power of the river was so great it lifted entire houses and dumped them downstream. It washed some away so completely that they vanished without a trace. Nearly 150 people were killed.

People still seem happy *to live beside the Big Thompson even though the damage was just a few years ago. Here houses have been rebuilt on the outside bend of a river – the most dangerous place of all.*

This house was carried many metres downstream *before it was stopped by the bridge. Notice how the bed is strewn with the large pebbles that did all the damage.*

This hillslope has recently been stripped of its trees *so that people can have fuelwood and land for animal grazing. Now storm waters will rush to rivers and cause flooding in the distant lowlands.*

At the mouth of the river Ganges *a vast delta is being built from the sediment washed from the Himalayan mountains. This is the land people are trying to reclaim for farming. But the rivers also bring frequent floods and many people are left homeless and their crops ruined.*

Cause and effect

In developing countries, rivers and lakes are often crucial as a water supply, and a source of irrigation water. People are often under such pressure to survive but governments do so little effective planning that river and lake environments suffer terribly.

In many developing countries every part of the landscape is used, from the highest peak to the ocean's edge. The result has been great changes in the natural flow of the rivers, changes which make the lives of many people even more miserable than they were in the past.

The hills and mountains of many rivers have been stripped of their trees in the last three decades. Trees have the ability to hold the soil and to let the rainwater seep into the ground. But as these have been removed, when it rains much of the water flows too quickly down to the rivers. As a result rivers are swollen much more often than in the past and people near to the river's mouth frequently experience the most dreadful flooding and many lose their lives.

Perilous homes

Flooding would be less important if it were not that huge numbers of people crowd on to the lowest-lying and most dangerous land beside rivers. They are forced to these places because there is simply no room elsewhere.

On rivers with strongly seasonal flows people are tempted to use the river bed for everything from drying washing to cultivating plants or building their homes.

As new waves of people migrate *from the countryside to cities they are forced to use every scrap of land for living. The shanty dwellers living on the floor of this river in the dry season work as servants in the distant skyscrapers. With no money for fares the people are forced to live close to their work but there is no other space in the city.*

A shanty is a settlement that houses the poorest people*, those least able to look after themselves in times of need. Nevertheless they have been forced to build out over this river to find a home. They risk being flooded every rainy season.*

7: A FUTURE FOR RIVERS?

One of the cheapest methods of transporting heavy goods *is by barges like the one shown here on Germany's River Rhine. To keep a sufficient depth of water for these river monsters requires constant dredging. In many cases the river can be encouraged to scour its own bed by forcing the current into a narrow central channel using training walls that jut out from the river banks.*

As more and more people live close to rivers, either through choice or necessity, there is a temptation to want to mould the river to human needs – to tame the rivers. People see that they need rivers for drinking, for irrigation, for transport, for power, and for recreation. People also want to live safely beside rivers, not be frightened by the prospect of flooding and death. The problem is trying to achieve all these objectives. Should engineers be given the charge of putting rivers in 'straight jackets' of concrete and steel or is there a better, cheaper and more sensitive way? The answers to how to use rivers and lakes depends on how much we choose to care for our environment.

Very large numbers of reservoirs *have been created in the world. Some are for drinking water, others for irrigation and yet others to hold back flood waters.*

Some reservoirs flood areas many thousands of square kilometres in size. All create new banks in which wildlife must struggle to regain a footing. They can be helped by combing down the bank to make ledges where water plants can easily grow. This is an expensive solution rarely adopted.

***Hydro-electric power plants**, like this one at Niagara on the Canadian/ US border, force the river to flow according to the daily routine of people. At times of high electricity demand, such as during the evening, large amounts of water are released through the turbines. At times of low demand, such as early in the morning, the river is reduced to a trickle.*

***In some places rivers change** from high to low flow very dramatically. The way the natural environment copes is by flooding. But when such a river flows through a city like San Jose, California, USA, it presents a major conflict between nature and people. The answer to this small river has been to case it in concrete. It may be functional but so much of beauty has been sacrificed to produce this stormwater drain.*

***The people who came to live in these houses wanted a river view** and a place to moor their boats. The engineers accomplished this by cutting the bank of the river and putting in reinforcements. Then they dredged the river bed to make sure there was deep enough water for the boats. This process of tidying up has completely removed the natural riverside environment. Grass, trees and soil have been replaced by concrete and steel. It may look nice, but it is a much more **sterile** place than before the developers came.*

Developing disaster

The problems in the developing world are strikingly different from those of the industrial countries. They nearly all stem from the way people use the river directly for so many things: from drinking to burying their dead.

The most important task is to improve the quality of the water by reducing the way it is used. Many rivers are hazardous to health simply because they are the daily repositories of human and animal waste. There is little industrial control and everyone, from the poorest bleacher to the largest industrial company, uses the river as a cheap way of getting rid of their waste.

Caring for developing world rivers means building water treatment plants and providing clean reliable piped supplies of water that everyone can use. But the cost of doing this is prohibitive and so, at the moment, there is little chance of improving water quality.

Another major task is to try to reforest the uplands and in this way control the floods that have begun to be a plague

Rivers are a source of livelihood *to many people on the River Yamuna near India's famous Taj Mahal. In this picture you can see people washing clothes, farming, taking cattle for water, living in huts (and using the water for drinking supplies). With such a diversity of uncontrolled use there is little chance of the river quality improving.*

***In the developing world** many people have no access to proper sewage plants or rubbish bins. As a result many rivers have been turned into sewers that are hazardous to the heath of all who live by them. The first requirement to improve such environments is an efficient waste management system.*

to all those living beside rivers. This is an easier task to put in to effect because it requires far less money than providing clean water. The people who cause reforestation are being shown cheap ways of replanting their hills so they do not lose valuable farmland but gain extra forest. The only cost is the provision of seedling trees and educating the people in the best ways of treating their lands.

***While people still bleach clothes** and let other harmful chemicals enter rivers like India's Yamuna, there is little hope that the river environment can be improved.*

Are we caring enough?

One way to find out how well people in the richer countries are caring for our environment is to conduct a series of surveys to show the quality of the water. This diagram shows the balance between good and bad water quality in the rivers and lakes of England and Wales, a region which is typical for most industrial countries. Since 1958 there has been a marked improvement in the worst polluted rivers (shown in red). They are mostly near to the sea in places used for ports and heavy industry.

Nevertheless, there are still some areas where no river life is possible and which are a danger to public health. Most bad rivers in 1958 had been improved only to poor quality (shown in yellow). The percentage of really healthy rivers has not improved at all because the sewage plants in some areas are becoming worn out and they do not work as well as in the past. Indeed, many people fear that the percentage of healthy rivers might get even smaller if old worn out sewage treatment plants are not replaced soon.

There is clearly a lot more that can be done to care for the river environment and make rivers healthy and good for plants, wildlife and people. It is perfectly possible to work with rivers and lakes, rather than to abuse them. It does not cost more and the benefits are far greater.

The starting point is to understand how rivers and lakes work, and how they are used by wildlife. Then their natural benefits can be used to give a more pleasant environment. The benefits are endless.

CLASSIFICATION OF RIVER QUALITY	
Category	**Current potential use**
Good quality	Healthy rivers and lakes where animals and plants flourish and which people can safely use for all purposes
Fair quality	Rivers and lakes that can be used for drinking water if they are properly treated. Wildlife still fairly frequent but the water cannot be safely used for all purposes.
Poor quality	Rivers and lakes in which most animals and plants cannot live. Unsuitable for recreation. The water can be used for industrial use only and cannot be made safe for drinking.
Bad quality	Water that is so polluted that no fish can survive and which can be a danger to public health.

1990

2% bad

8% poor

22% fair

72% good

68% good

1958

7% bad

7% poor

14% fair

Poor areas *still occur near to places where there is heavy industry lining river banks. It includes places where spillage from tankers are loading and unloading or where accidents frequently send polluting substances into the rivers.*

Older industrial areas *still often do not rate better than poor. A lot of work still has to be done to improve sewage works and to make sure that factory treatment plants are modernized.*

Many city centres *are based around rivers. As heavy industry and docks close down and move away, so the city authorities get the chance to improve the river environment with parks and gardens. With less industry the water quality automatically improves.*

The open countryside *is still mainly a place where water quality is good, largely because it is under-developed. The main problems occur when fertilizers seep from the fields into rivers and lakes.*

GLOSSARY

abrade
the gradual wearing away of rocks as they bounce against one another. Abrasion will gradually reduce large stones to sand sized pieces which are easy for the river to carry away

aquatic
a term used to describe animals and plants that live in water

aquifer
a rock which has either pores or fissures that allow water to move through it. Most rocks have some water in, but only limestones and sandstones hold enough water to be useful for irrigation

cataracts
large sequences of rapids that occur where hard rock bands reduce the ability of the river to cut down into the bed

creep
the slow downhill movement of soil due to wetting and drying. Whenever rain falls it wets the soil and the soil particles swell. Then, as the soil dries out the soil shrinks again. Each swelling and shrinking cycle moves soil an imperceptible distance downslope

ecosystem
the stable mix of plants and animals that can survive in an area. An ecosystem can be as small as a pond or as large as a rainforest

eddies
the swirling movement of water as it flows against a river bank or bed. Eddies are important because they can whisk particles from the bed and into the fastest flowing regions of water in the middle of the channel. Here they are more easily carried away

flashy
a river that rises and falls quickly in response to a storm. The most flashy rivers are those where the soils are clays and where water cannot easily soak into the soil

habitat
a habitat contains just the right kind of soil, moisture, shelter and climate in which a plant or animal can best thrive.

herbivores
plant eating animals. These animals convert plant materials into meat and they are the food for the carnivores

moraine
the material deposited by a glacier at the limits of its influence. Terminal moraines are often left by glaciers across mountain valleys at the end of an Ice Age, damming any rivers and forming lakes

reach
a stretch of a river that has similar characteristics

sediment
the material carried by a river. The finest sediment is called clay and this is responsible for muddying floodwaters. Larger sizes of sediment are called silt, sand, gravel, pebbles and boulders respectively

soil pores
the tiny gaps that naturally occur in a soil between the soil particles

sterile environment
an environment which has less variety than that which occurred in the natural state

INDEX